Journey to Empowerment

Stories of women who rose to find their voice

Tiffanie
Davis

Lynéa
Laws

Yvonne
Mahoney

Journey to Empowerment
Stories of Women Who Rose to Find Their Voice

By
Tiffanie Davis, Lynéa Laws and Yvonne Mahoney

Published by
Meet the World Image Solutions

www.mtwimagesolutions.com

Cover design by Dr. Rhonda M. Lawson

ISBN:
979-8-9872429-5-7
Meet the World Image Solutions

Contents

Foreword

I was truly honored when Dr. Laws asked me to write the foreword. We have been friends for more than fifteen years.

Her purpose for asking me to write the foreword was simple: I was the first. The first president of the first four-letter chapter of Zeta Phi Beta Sorority, Incorporated in the state of Georgia and the Southeastern Region – Alpha Alpha Kappa Zeta chapter. This honor has never been something I have taken lightly. It seems like yesterday that ten years ago, this amazing chapter was chartered. Thank you. Thank you to the ladies who stepped out to create the chapter, and to those who have continued to expand the vision of the chapter ten years later.

I started this foreword and was pulled away from it by my seven-week-old daughter. As I sat in the dark rocking her and patiently watching her fight to stay awake, I realized she is symbolically every woman whom I have ever come across in some way. She's a fighter. My baby was fighting sleep, and symbolically, I was the world. In some ways, I was there to comfort her, guide her, and to push her in the right direction (going to sleep). In other ways, I was just like the demands she will face as she ages.

I needed her to go to sleep right then, not on her schedule. At this age, little people make their own rules, and mommies have to follow them, not the other way around.

Why is that important? Because this is just one glimpse into the lives and stories that encompass this book. My story is no greater than the amazing stories on the pages that follow.

It is often said that women are mothers, caregivers, girlfriends, wives, and sisters. We sometimes forget that we are also storytellers, listeners, and whispers of wisdom and truth.

Kudos to the ladies who participated in the chapter's Women Empowerment Cohort. Congratulations for staying the course and using the cohort to chase better, bravely speak your truth, find healing, and strive toward authentically and freely living each day. I applaud you.

Within the pages of this book, all of this comes out. As you read, remember to take time to reflect on the stories while reflecting on your own situations in life. The pages of this book are but a glimpse into the lives of the writers. You, as a reader, are embarking on a journey of healing, love, laughter, joy, pain, sadness, and, most of all, revelation.

Enjoy it.

Live in the moment.

Hopefully, you will be inspired to create your own book of stories for a generation to come.

With Love,

Terri N. Bell, Ph.D.

Introduction

In the age of empowerment, where the resounding voices of women echo through corridors long dominated by patriarchy, a beacon of change emerges. Welcome to the Women Empowerment Cohort, a sanctuary where women gather to explore, define, and manifest their empowerment.

This anthology stands as a testament to these ladies' transformative journeys. The Women Empowerment Cohort, initiated by Zeta Phi Beta Sorority, Incorporated, Alpha Alpha Kappa Zeta Chapter in Newnan, Georgia, embodies the sorority's principles of scholarship, service, sisterhood, and finer womanhood, particularly service and finer womanhood. While society often prioritizes judging women based on appearance, the sorority's concept of finer womanhood transcends superficiality. It centers on women empowering themselves and others, finding joy in community upliftment and fostering sisterly bonds. These women set high standards, embrace growth, and continuously refine themselves.

Service is the bedrock of the organization, resonating strongly with its members' values. Women often instinctively prioritize caring for others, sometimes losing sight of their own needs and goals in the process. Thus, the Cohort's purpose was to refocus and bolster women's self-esteem, goals, vision, leadership skills, and succession planning, guiding them toward becoming distinguished Finer Women. Amidst the camaraderie of the shared experiences, these women explored the realms of self-discovery, entrepreneurship, education, and leadership. This is a chronicle of their collective wisdom, resilience, and unwavering determination.

At the heart of their gatherings lay an exploration of what women's empowerment truly entails. Through workshops and discussions, they questioned preconceived notions, dismantled societal constructs, and embraced the multifaceted nature of empowerment. They discussed not only what it means to be empowered as women, but also what it means to empower women collectively.

Central to this journey was the realization that empowerment begins with self-awareness. Thus, each woman embarked on a journey of self-discovery to understand her strengths, her passions, and her purpose. This introspection served as the cornerstone upon which each participant built her path to empowerment.

One of the pivotal themes of discussion revolved around financial independence. Through the exploration of strategies to cultivate seven streams of income, women reclaimed their economic agency to brainstorm ways to forge new pathways to prosperity.

Empowerment, we learned, is not only about breaking glass ceilings but also about building sturdy foundations from which to soar.

In the pursuit of empowerment, the journey of learning is perpetual. The ladies embraced the ethos of continuing education, recognizing that knowledge is not static, but rather a river that flows endlessly.

Moreover, they explored the realm of organizational management and insights necessary to lead with purpose and efficacy.

Yet, beyond the workshops and discussions lies the true essence of this endeavor – the stories of women who dared to dream, to act, and to inspire. This anthology is a direct result of their courage, their resilience, and their unwavering commitment to change. Through these narratives, we invite you to witness the transformative power of women telling their stories and taking action.

As you immerse yourself in these pages, may you be moved, inspired, and empowered. Within these stories lies the promise of a future where every woman is free to soar, to lead, and to shape her destiny.

Letters of Love

By
Tiffanie Davis

This chapter is dedicated to my ancestors. Because of you, I AM.

Love, Tiffanie

The Early Years

Dear Beloved,

I met you for the first time today, although I've known you forever. You are a beautiful sight to behold, but you don't know it yet. You are still hiding the magnificent parts of you that make you unique. I've seen you walk the hall with your head held down. It makes it hard to grab a glance of your wide and expressive eyes. When you do look up and our eyes meet, they speak to me without you having to say a word. I know we are divinely connected. I feel your soul.

I'm not able to reveal myself to you until the time is right. Until then, accept my letters of love from my heart to yours.

Sincerely,
An Admirer

Sunday, March 6, 1988

Dear Diary,

It's been a hard day. My emotions are all over the place. The comparison-itis moments were tough. At church today, a mother came up to me and said, "Honey, you would be so beautiful, if you weren't so BIG. I have a VHS video of Richard Simmons doing some exercises you can do at home and a scale so you can weigh your food. I'm praying for you, baby."

Are you serious?!?!?!!??

My eyes began to sweep the fellowship hall. Over by the Coke machine was Tina, the granddaughter of the mother who said she was "praying for me" about my weight. She's only a year older than me, but her body tells a different story. Chocolate, smooth skin, thick in the "right" places, and, as a result, the center of attention, especially with boys. As I continued to glance around the fellowship hall, I realized I was literally the largest person in the room. AGAIN.

Invisible, yet sticking out like a sore thumb. Why is this my existence? I can hear my mother's voice, the

Elder, in my head, "An answer to everything is found in the Bible."

Well, Let's see…

Psalms 139

Oh Lord, You've searched me and know me
Tell me, what do you see?
Because when I look at myself,
I feel so unhappy.
Why do I look so fat?
Why is my voice so loud?
Why did this happen to me?
Couldn't you have given me her style?
You said I am fearfully and wonderfully made,
But I see contradictions
With what I have been given.
So, Lord, I come to you now
For an explanation.
Please give a revelation.
I don't understand
Why I can't be like someone else.
What is your plan?
Please help me understand.

*****

Dear Diary,

Big Momma just called me to come to the kitchen to eat, and in normal "Big Momma" fashion, her announcements made me feel like I'm in the way, and WRONG. I wasn't the one who used her lunch meat, but her fussy tone always makes me feel just as guilty as if I had. Say something back? Absolutely not! I'm fully aware of the irritated tone that would continue should I say anything that might suggest that SHE is wrong. This is a daily occurrence. We don't interact much. When we do, it makes me feel like more of a nuisance and bother to her. The "announcements" seem to be her grievances with us, but she never discusses them with us directly. As a result, I spend most of my time out of the way, alone, in my room.

You are my friend. You never talk back to me, but you get all of the emotions, thoughts, feelings, actions, and reactions that I need to sort out. My mother and I would discuss our experiences living in the same house with her mother and father and how Big Momma's hardened exterior made us feel. Neither of us do well with confrontation, especially when it deals with Big Momma. When she was here, our talk times felt more like sisters than mother-daughter. That could be due to our only fifteen-year age gap. She really is my best friend. I miss the conversations with her. Momma got married last year and moved out with her husband. Now she's pregnant with my little sister. Since she moved out, I'm here with Big Momma alone. So you, diary, get all of the experiences that I can't talk to anyone else about.

Thank you for hearing me, seeing me, and accepting me just as I am.

*****

Dear Beloved,

I know you spend many nights in your room with your thoughts, feeling alone. You've never said it out loud, but I know living with your grandparents makes you feel put away, unseen, and unheard. As a matter of fact, you sometimes think your mom, your closest friend, escaped the scrutiny and dismissiveness of your grandmother once she got married. Here you are, left to deal (or not) with her alone. You avoid her as much as humanly possible. If you say very little so she won't fuss, but "announcements" are made that you know are indirectly about you. The announcements plague your thoughts. I know how they cause you to retreat into your room, back into your shell, back to those inner musings that play in your mind like a song on repeat. You are young, so it's hard for you to understand and fathom that these experiences make your heart so palatable yet build strength in you. It's this that builds the empathy and compassion that you display genuinely to everyone you meet. Eventually you will see what I see in you: pure love for others that is priceless and beautiful.

Sincerely,
Your Admirer

*****

Dear Diary,

We just made it back home from the grocery store. Of course, I'm playing the tape of songs I recorded from the radio and the smooth voice of Luther Vandross is singing *Here and Now*. They make me think about my phone song battles with Ahmad. Ahmad and I have known each other since we were five years old, and even back then, the adults wanted us to "go together". His mother and mine are friends and sometimes we ended up at each other's house after church. He was my first kiss, and yes, that kiss happened at church.

But here I am now, thinking about us on the phone late at night because we had to make sure everyone in the house was "down" for the night. We would talk about what happened at church and at school, recapping the letters we secretly wrote to each other because only our closest friends knew we were a thing. At school, I could only steal a gaze or two of Ahmad, hoping his eyes would at least catch mine. At least there I could see we were a couple. Outside of the little interactions we would have at church, school was even more off limits.

"Oh, that's a good one," Ahmad said after I played *Make it Like It Was* by Regina Belle. "But I got you with this one!"

Then played *Goodbye Love* by Guy. The song battle would continue well after midnight, until we had both fallen asleep on the phone and eventually woke up long enough to hang up.

Tonight, all of that is just a memory. I wrote him a letter today and gave it to my friend Sam to give to him in third period. I couldn't stay focused in my literature class, wondering if he had read the letter and if he would write me back. Sometimes he doesn't and I'm left wondering. Our school interactions are few and far between. And this letter expressed just that. I want him to know that I love him. I know why our relationship is secret. I don't want or need him to say it or write it.

My heart aches as Luther's voice continues. I remember the letter that I got from Ahmad after fourth period, saying it was over – again. Ugh! I hate that I'm crying. But I want so badly for someone to love me. I wish we could be like the couples I see walking in the hallway holding hands. I wanted to be like the girls who got one of the huge cookie cakes from Great American Cookie Company and balloons for Valentine's. I wanted us to be "Amina and Ahmad", the couple where when you saw one, the other was right there. That was not us, nor has it ever been me. I fade into the background at school, hoping for a glance my way, and sometimes even *that* passes me by. He doesn't want anyone to know, and that hurts. Will I ever be needed, desired, wanted and loved like what I see around me?

The enemy inside me taunts me, tells me it can't be. Your dreams, wants and desires

Will continue to be a mystery. The love you seek will never be. Who could love someone like me?

*****

Dear Beloved,

You are worth more than being someone's secret. You deserve to be loved out loud, fully, wholly and completely! Both of you are young. And in his young mind, his reputation means more to him than you do. I noticed the longing in your face when you saw him passing in the hallway. Yes, PASSING! No conversation, no acknowledgement, just a stare and you both move on to class. I know your heart breaks each time this happens, and then Valentine's Day rolls around and you see the other girls with balloons, cookie cakes, wearing their boyfriends' Starter jackets, walking together to class. And you barely get a stare. God forbid someone sees him looking your way, then he too would be the brunt of the jokes. Talking to the fat girl. One day you both will realize what truly matters and what love really looks and feels like.

With the love you long for,
Your Admirer

Saturday, October 1, 1988

Dear Diary,

It's my thirteenth birthday! My dad came by today and gave me some Gloria Vanderbilt perfume and a violin. His gifts have always included something musical. But this time, I didn't have the heart to tell him I haven't played the violin since fifth grade (now I'm in seventh). He doesn't come around much. He comes over sometimes on holidays, my birthday, and maybe one or two random days every other year or so.

Clearly, my love for music comes from him. When he comes, our time together is anchored in music. He always wanted to listen to music and sing with me. I can remember his love for Chaka Khan and how he insisted I write her a letter on his behalf. I used to do the same with Michael Jackson. You could see the imprint of my letters if you held up the *Off the Wall* album cover at just the right angle because I used to write my letters on top of it.

Oh, I did receive my usual card from my grandmother that had a dollar for each year of my age. I had the typical birthday cake, birthday song, and then music in my room. Since I have this violin, I might as well take it out and see what I can remember from playing in fifth grade.

Tween, Teen & In-between

June 1, 1991

Dear Diary,

Lorenzo heard me singing in the hallway to myself at Upward Bound today. I thought I was alone, but I could hear a faint voice speak over the sound of Keith Staten's verse in *Back in the Saddle*.

"So, you can sing."

"A little, mostly at church though," I responded, removing the headphones of my walkman from my ears.

"Who are you listening to?" "Commissioned."

"I've heard of them before." "It's their latest album."

This exchange was different from any other I had experienced, especially nothing like what I had with Ahmad. Although we were the only ones in the hallway at the time, I didn't feel like he was ashamed to be seen talking to me. He later sat across from me in the multi-purpose room where all classes would come together. I could feel him watching me. He asked me a few questions as we sat listening to Ms. Davis, the Upward Bound program manager, talk to us about our upcoming college tour to Xavier University in New Orleans and Texas Southern University later this summer. Lorenzo even asked me if I planned to go.

"Not sure," I said with a shoulder shrug.

"I hope you decide to," he said with a grin and a certain gleam in his eye that I never saw from Ahmad, or anyone for that matter.

"Can we exchange numbers so you can let me know what you decide?"

Wait, What!?! Did he just ask me for my number? Of course, I gave it to him. Let's see if he actually calls.

*****

October 1991

Dear Diary,

I know it's been a minute. After the phone number exchange, Lorenzo and I talked on the phone often. I did decide to go on the Upward Bound field trip, and he even asked me to sit with him on the bus.

On the trip, Lorenzo and I got closer. I couldn't believe that he asked me to sit with him! He even did little things that made me feel special the entire trip, like holding my hand and putting his arm around me. For the first time ever, someone showed interest in me and didn't seem to mind that other people knew. We did take some opportunities on the trip that didn't make God proud, but I enjoyed every bit of them. He even asked me to come on a local trip with his church to a park. With that trip, we became even closer.

This feels like love. We connect over music in a different way than I did with Ahmad. Our "song battles" are the same, but the discussions we have about the music are rich and deep. We get lost in talking about Commissioned and their beautiful harmonies. We lightly debate our theories of why they are number 1 in the category of Contemporary Gospel Male Groups. And we grieve that they are rarely recognized as the greats they are. Sometimes we stop and sing those special parts in the song where the harmony gets good. You know that part when you have to close your eyes and direct the moves of the specific voice part (alto) that hits your soul in that just right spot. And after I sing, sometimes Lorenzo says, "Your voice is so beautiful." I swear I melt inside every time.

Let me catch you up a bit, Diary. Lorenzo is a rapper—a gospel rapper—and he sometimes shares pieces of music he's working on with me. I become mesmerized by his flow and his lyrics stimulate my mind. When we are on the phone and he raps, I hum, and maybe even add in a rhyme to a hook here or there. In those moments, it's collaborative and intimate. We are officially together, and I LOVE US!

It feels so right. Could he be the one?

November 1991

Amina,

So, your usual phone call with him turned into THE breakup call. You reveled in the calls every morning. Someone was genuinely interested in you, and this time, wasn't afraid for others to know. A spiritually connected, lover of music, just like you. The conversations, the touches, the time spent together, the kisses, and the other all began to feel like lies.

It felt like a dream to you, but on the phone call this morning, he told you he's still in love with his ex.

Immediately, you feel like the rebound, the *has been*, never quite enough to compare to her. She is the slender-framed, light-skinned beauty from a well-known connected family in the church scene, which in your world, *is* the world. He apologized, you remained calm, accepting even, and all the while believing he never really felt anything real for you. Instead, he was looking for a replacement, and you were the convenient, easy alternative. The rebound.

Those words continued to play over and over in your head all the way to school. In your heart, the comparisons to her and those like her continued. All you could see around you were "the beautiful ones", so blind to how beautiful you really were. Oblivious to the shining spirit that you have that pulls those who thought not to engage with you, to do the opposite.

It was completely HIS LOSS. But for you, depression settles in. You shrink yourself into the shadows of inner darkness. You lessen that natural shine because of your uniqueness. Not truly realizing that the beauty you naturally possess may never be within the reach of those you compare yourself to. The you, you are authentically, is the you I long to be with. Others may never get it, but I certainly hope that soon you will.

With true love,
Your Admirer

Adult-ish

October 2007

My Beloved Amina,

Yes, he is a wonderful man, but this relationship was more about you. You hurt him with your decisions, but you learned more about yourself. You knew from the moment you said yes to him that you were really saying no to yourself. Getting married felt like the right thing to do, the natural conventional course of action when you have dated for years. Ending the marriage was messy, but necessary for your growth.

As you sit by this lake at the monastery writing prayers and contemplating your next steps, understand that your power is in your pen. Know that when you write, I write.

Love,
Your Secret Admirer

Amina,

It all traces back to your childhood. You're thirty-five now and reflecting on the decisions you made in your twenties to early thirties. These are moments we can all relate to. Those times when we made some "not-so-good" decisions. Decisions that reveal a character you never really tried to hide but were perceived to be by your introverted nature. Humans have perceptions based on their own perspective. Those perceptions can be toxic. Hence, the birthplace of your issues with perfectionism, steeped in a soup of Black Church.

The range of what life offered you in this phase of your life were your growing pains. Yes, you hurt yourself and others, but eventually, you will look back at these moments and understand though they were UGLY, it was necessary for your growth.

Still admiring YOU,
Your Secret Love

April 4th, 2011

Dear Diary,

So much has happened since I last wrote. I believe I've truly found my person. It all started with one look at the party my friend dragged me to, and here we are today, only a few short months later, committing our lives to each other forever.

What's the difference, you ask? One, we started as friends before anything physical. Secondly, I ultimately listened to my heart and took a chance on unconventional love. I came back to you today, Diary, because I have to write out my wedding vows. For some reason, whenever I write to you, everything gets clear and creative juices flow, so here goes…

Who Knew?

Who knew that you would come into my life,
Changing my world, making my dark days bright?

Who knew that you

would bring a love so sweet,

And that you would want to give that love to only me?

A love so amazing, so real, so true, A love that takes my
breath away, Turning my gray skies blue.

You came out of my dreams,

Making them reality.

Brought me joy and happiness That I never
thought could be.

I pledge to you my heart today, filled with uncondi-
tional love, Promising to stick and stay

As we continue to be blessed from above.

Forever, will I love you And give to you my all,

Wanting you always in my corner To be there
when I fall.

Ronni, you are my love, my everything, My all, my life.

I stand before you this day, Proud to BE and to call
you My WIFE.

Discovery

September 13, 2013

Dear Momma,

I know that this is going to be one of the hardest letters I write. It's your birthday, but also your homegoing. It's hard to believe I've lost you. I often think about the fact that I gave you the money to go on the trip, and wonder if I hadn't, would you still be here?

I think about the day I got the call. I can still see it in my mind. I had just walked from my class to Art. I had gotten back to my classroom and joined my teammates in a discussion. I began to tell the story of the last five days of my pregnancy leading up to losing Elijah at twenty-one weeks pregnant. As I told the story, my eyes began to well with tears, full of all of the *what ifs*. What if I had him? What would he be like now? Would he love music like me or have his daddy's eyes? I even shared with them the plans we made for you to keep him after he was born so I could save on daycare.

A few minutes later, I got the call. Ronni was on her way to pick me up from work to take me to you. I will never forget the ride to where you were, the calls I made trying to find out if you were alright. The minute I got closer and saw the lights of the fire trucks in the distance, my stomach sank. I immediately knew.

Now that you're gone, I realize more and more how you were my best friend. We would fall out, go a while not talking to each other, and then I'd get a call. We would talk like all was well and never address what we were mad about. After a while, the sting of the thing would fade away in our memories and love always remained.

I wish we had talked after the house fire. I wish I could have heard your thoughts now about my relationship. I believe the fire was divine. It was meant for you to live with us and to see that she genuinely loves me. You asked me once, "Is she like that all the time?" I knew it was because you witnessed how she extravagantly cares for me and loves me fully. For the first time ever, I could confidently answer, "Absolutely" because I know she does. Did it change how you saw our relationship? I guess now that's one of the things I'll never find out.

I see you in myself. I find myself recognizing you in the way I laugh, organize, and seek knowledge. I felt you really strong last week while I was vacuuming and singing. I felt you, Big Momma, and my great-grandmother, Muh. I immediately began to feel stronger with every note, and wiser with every push of the vacuum. Thank you for that moment, and the moments since when you come to me in my dreams.

I am because *you were*. Words truly can't express how much I treasure our relationship. It wasn't perfect, but it was ours, and you are the fabric of my being. I'm forever grateful for the opportunity I had to tell you how much you meant to me on Mother's Day a few months before you passed.

You will always be my bestest friend!

Love,
Amina

March 1, 2020

Dear Diary,

Last night, I reunited with an old friend. We go waaay back. It had been years since we talked, but we picked up as if no time had passed. Spending time with her last night was refreshing. She listened intently and shared her wisdom at just the right moment.

She wondered why we hadn't connected in so long, and why, when we would try to connect, life would get in the way.

Many people would tell me to reach out to her, but I allowed time and obligations to get in the way of truly reaching out although she was always on my mind.

See, she was there for me in some of the hardest moments of my life, and she never judged me. She never left me when things got tough.

Last night's reunion reminded me how much I'd missed her. Honestly, I didn't know how much I've needed her.

I have to promise myself to maintain this precious connection, to cultivate it, and I'm sure she will be there for me as she always has been.

Thank you and welcome back, Pen.

April 16, 2020

Dear Diary,

There have been some major changes in my world. A major one being COVID-19. Right now, we are in week five of sheltering in place and working from home.

Initially, this change for me has squared more with my personality as an introvert. I have enjoyed the flexibility and comfort it affords me. However, there have been some other adjustments that haven't been as pleasant.

In recent months, I have noticed a pattern of feeling dismissed and unheard. In the truest nature of an introvert, I try hard to reflect on what it is and what it says about me and my make up without projecting my issues on the other person. This week, this problem became increasingly more difficult. Why, you ask? Because there's no escape when you're quarantined at home!

This time when I expressed myself, it was connected to my own fears, so it hurt much worse when they were ignored. Not only ignored, but it was also said that I never even said ANYTHING!!! What?!?!? Of course, this sent my thoughts into a downward spiral. As one who tries to analyze and reflect, my thoughts consumed me, and my usual peace escaped me. I succumbed to the loss

of control over my situation and viewed it as a perma-
nent sentence on the demise of my voice. Why are my
thoughts dismissed? Why are my ideas stifled? Do I not
matter? Is what I'm thinking stupid? Why am I so alone
in my thoughts, views, and perspectives?

As I have progressed through this week, I have employed
a diverse number of coping strategies, one of which is
getting back to writing. I have tried to make sure I didn't
overindulge in self-destructive behaviors that will do me
more harm than good. Did I indulge in a few things?
YES! A drink (or three), a smoke, or chocolate ice cream,
yep, and they all felt great. But I knew I couldn't live
there. Riding my stationary bike, prayer, starting a new
Bible plan, texting my therapist, sitting on the porch,
listening to music, reading instructional books are a few
of the ways I've tried to calm my mind and deal with the
thoughts in my head.

Introverts don't like to talk. Don't get me wrong, I will,
but it's not my first drug of choice to deal with life. Too
much "people-ing" depletes me. Being alone recharges
me. I understand that about myself now.

However, a conversation today with a very intuitive soul
was extremely helpful. It's amazing how when I started
to share things, the answer began to surface within me
before I could finish my statement.

Here is what I learned:

1. **Release the expectation I place on others.** Many times, when I share my thoughts, feelings, ideas, and perspectives, there is the expectation that it will be understood and acted upon. Not everyone is prepared and ready to receive my message. No matter how much I try to "speak the truth in love", the receiver just may not be mentally, emotionally, or spiritually ready to act. There are some days (and some people with which) I can do this very well. It is quite difficult when it's with those with whom you share space daily. That takes intentional practice.

1b. **Minimal expectations, minimal disappointment.** This is much like the first (hence 1b). I have told myself this before, and it used to be my mantra, but clearly, I needed a brutal reminder this week.

2. **To break a pattern, go back to the root.** I have noticed that this dismissed, unheard feeling continues to rear its ugly head in my life in different people and forms. I have to dig and figure out the source of this feeling. What relationship in my past/childhood is mimicked in these instances that caused me to feel unheard and dismissed? As I thought about this during our conversation, my grandmother was the first relationship that bubbled up for me. My father was the second. I'm certain

as I continue to write, the significance of those stories will increase. Then, the relationship with myself
came up. *That* very well may be the root. As I write
that, my eyes begin to well, and the butterflies begin
to rage in my stomach. I believe the root has just
been dug up!

3. **Stop Saving People.** I'm a helper by default, in some cir-
cles, some may say I'm an empath or healer. It's in my nature to alleviate what ails others. At times this is fine,
but other times, it's enabling. When others reach out
for answers, I have to say, "We are all human and we
all experience things differently. As a result, I may
not have all the answers for you and your situation.
I encourage you to reflect and think about what the
best option for you may be that you can live with."
After that, I need to refer back to number one!

May this entry be a step in my journey of living, loving,
and learning while I process being fully, wholly ME.

June 1, 2020

Dear Big Momma,

Happy belated birthday! I have been thinking and processing a lot leading up to your day, much of which has helped me understand more about the reasons for who I am growing to be. I'm often reminded of you now in my adulthood in various forms, and I'm certain now that I can learn from our relationship.

Let me begin with a thank you. I appreciate you for creating a stable home for me with you and Big Daddy before and after my mother married my sister's father. You and Big Daddy maintained normalcy for me during my preteen to teenage years. You both provided food, shelter, and necessities for me. Physically, all my needs were met. Again, thank you.

Mentally, however, my experience was a bit different. I can remember from an early age that communication between us was very little. Many times, I felt as if I was a bother to you. Momma would often say she felt the same. Conversation was relegated to subliminal announcements about what wasn't going right. Any conversation outside of that or about church felt taboo.

As I review my childhood, I'm reminded that I was

conceived when Momma was very young. I can imagine now how that must have hurt you. I can imagine you may have felt like it may have been something you did or didn't do that caused it to happen. How angry you must have been with my mother. I'm sure that was hard to deal with. Seeing me every day, having to provide for both me and Mom, had to be a reminder of those feelings. As you distanced yourself from Momma, you were even further distanced from me. And I felt it every day. This lack of emotional connection permeated through the relationships in our family, between you and Big Daddy, you and Momma, and you and me. As a result, I have always felt a sense of rejection. This rejection spilled over into my personal views of myself. With no real tools to combat those who would bully me about my weight, inside and outside the family, I developed a comparison complex, feeling and believing that I wasn't enough and doubting myself in every area.

I regret that it took so many years since you're passing to be able to relate to you and your story as a woman. This letter is a hard, yet necessary process of my internal healing. Even as I write this, your true intentions continue to be revealed despite the persona you portrayed. I understand now that this persona was because you felt it was needed; you weren't aware of any other way to be. Your repeated hurt caused you to retreat and sometimes lash out at those you loved because you weren't sure how to deal with it.

I intend to break this cycle. I intend to see YOU. To see you as disappointed, hurt, unsure, defensive, and even rejected. I also see you as strong, unique, and determined. I intend to see the love you were afraid to display. I will be your legacy of transparency, vulnerability, and compassion first to myself, and then to others.

I love you. Thank you for helping me grow, even from the other side. Through your shades of blue is me.

With love,
Amina

September 26, 2020

Dear Diary,

Since being quarantined and away from the hustle and bustle of church life, it has had me reflecting. I have to admit there has been a sense of freedom since I haven't *had* to be at church, especially being there to serve in music ministry. I've thought about the phrases I've heard like, "That wasn't 'of God'"; "You need to come before God 'holy boldness'"; "Release the 'sound of worship'"; "It's okay baby"; "Decent and in order"; and "spirit of excellence".

The average "church kid" has heard all of these phrases and then some. They often come from the church elite, who appear to be the epitome of the life that God deems worthy. Then after church, the verbiage changes: "She's at the altar every Sunday for prayer, bless her heart"; "They didn't look like they could sing a lick"; "Girl, did you see the skirt she was wearing today?"; "That note wasn't even on the keyboard"; and "It just didn't sit right in my spirit."

It wasn't until recently that I realized these phrases are the root of my *comparisonitis*.

The church is a major part of who I am. I was that kid

who was there with my mom every time the church doors opened. My first out of town trips, my friends, my childhood, my adulthood, my vocabulary, the phrasing of my writing, are all influenced by the church. I realize and admit that in my *churchiness*, I have said some of the same phrases. Upon reflection, these phrases can come off quite judgmental. The *churchy* way of correction has a form of 'love' but denies the power thereof (Again, my churchiness is ingrained. LOL)

Love: a word that sums up the life of Christ, yet when it comes to the "church", it isn't always evident. If there is one thing that sums up all of what is lacking in society, it's love. In its *genuine* form, it accepts differences, listens with the heart, is present in difficulty, is truthful, yet gentle, it protects, it builds up, and grows up.

In the last year, it has become more evident to me how inauthentic we can be with one another. Not that this hasn't been happening all along, but the "scales fell from my eyes" and it was blatant. So much so, that I constantly soul search and say to myself, "Don't be fake. Let your yea be yea, and your nay be nay in and out of the person's face."

During quarantine, I've felt safe from this. No need to put on this certain dress, smile this way, sing that way, pray, not to jiggle too much—wearing the right undergarments to prevent it—nor constantly ask myself,

"Was that enough?"; "Was that 'of God'?"; "Did I move too much?"; "Did I get into myself with that vocal run?"; "Did we sing too long?"; "Did they feel God?"; "Do we look okay?"; "What does he think?"; "Does she approve?"; or, when the "love" is given, walking away thinking, "I wonder what they're saying at the dinner table with their friends."

So hence another facet of my journey to complete self-acceptance, I've begun losing my "religion" and releasing the people to find ME.

January 2024

Dear Diary,

I'm having an overwhelming feeling of ME. It's something unexplainable, yet familiar. A freedom in this moment that is authentically who I am, but never have been. Of course, while I'm here at this moment, I had to pick up the pen and write, and you know what happens when I do…

ME

I'm so full of me right now,
I don't know where to begin.
Just full of who I am. The essence of me.

I don't know if this is a poem

or just an essay on the of ALL of me.
It is me…just ME.

Whew! It's so overwhelming to BE
In this moment in the IT of me,
that's what makes me, ME

INTIMACY, the IS of me.
LOVE, The who, what, where and when of ME.
The Sexy, Sassy, BE of ME.
Just Me, Wholly ME.

LOVE,
ME

*****

Amina,

I've been with you all along, although my letters to you
began before you recognized my presence. I was there

from the first kiss to the one whose kiss you will have forever. The love from Ronni was sent to you because it was necessary in order for us to be together. I was always your secret, admiring you from afar. Wanting to hear your voice, for you to talk to me. No fancy words necessary. Time with you is all I need. I want to tell you the plans I have for us. How we will work together. How my love for you is true and tender.

But you seem to have no time for me. I long for intimacy. Your time, your talent, your money all takes you away from me. There is so much I want to share with you, but you are so busy with work, the kids, and others. I tend to get lost in the shuffle of things, and you only think of me on occasion. I have so much to say to you, but I get lost in all you do. I promise if you give me the chance to love you, you will never go without.

The divine spirit within you is me, and we have loved you for your entire existence. Through the heartbreak, the mess ups, the doubt, the fear, and everything in between, the love you sought after was always there waiting for you to realize you had it all along. Maybe now you can see how everything was designed to bring you into YOU and that I was there waiting to love you all along.

Finally with self-love,
Amina

Acknowledgments

I am a proud member of Zeta Phi Beta Sorority, Incorporated, Alpha Alpha Kappa Zeta chapter, where I have served for six of my seven years as a Zeta. I appreciate our chapter president, Dr. Lynèa Laws, for the vision to empower us to embrace our own journeys through sharing our voice. Her vision has afforded me the opportunity to finally birth one of the books that had been brewing in my heart for a very long time. This was the push I needed. I am thankful for the support of my family, friends, and Sorors as I continue the journey embracing and celebrating all that's ME.

The Road Less Traveled

By

Dr. Lynéa Laws

To every woman who believed in Black Excellence and now seeks freedom of self. Live as your authentic self and be unapologetic.

To me.

The Phone Call

"Have you lost your mind?" my mother exclaimed, her tone incredulous. "I don't understand why you think moving across the water is necessary."

"Why do you feel the need to go over there?" my father interjected, his voice stern with concern. "You have no family there. It's dangerous. They kill people!"

Their words hit me like a wave, but I steadied myself, knowing I had to stand my ground.

"I hear your concerns," I replied calmly, trying to convey the strength of my conviction, "but this opportunity means everything to me. It's about more than just the job or the location—it's about the opportunity to do what I want to do for once instead of doing what society and family think I should be doing."

My mother's voice softened, tinged with sadness. "I understand. I wanted to travel, too, but Papa and Mama Laws forbade me to do so."

There was a pause on the other end of the line, and then my father spoke, his tone resigned. "You've always been determined. If this is what you truly want, we don't have a choice but to accept it. But we don't like it. Please be careful."

"I will. I'm going to wait to get the contract via email and read it over. They said if I'm not happy there, I can break my contract and come home. I'll follow up with more details on when I leave as soon as I know more."

And with that, we said our goodbyes, their disapproval echoing in my mind as I prepared to embark on this new chapter of my life.

As a southern girl raised in the heart of Baptist tradition, I was no stranger to the weight of authority and the importance of familial respect. In my family, what the elders said was gospel, and questioning it was unheard of. Disrespect was met with swift consequences—a stern lecture, the silent treatment, or a slap across the mouth to remind you of your place.

When I broached the subject of my decision to move to a foreign land for a job, I knew I was treading on thin ice. My parents' reaction was exactly as I had anticipated—shock, disbelief, and an underlying current of disappointment. They couldn't fathom why I would go against their wishes, why I would risk venturing into the unknown when safety and familiarity lay within my home country.

Yet, as I reflected on their loud silence, I couldn't help but feel a sense of déjà vu. After all, I was already pushing the envelope by residing in a different state, separated from both my immediate and extended family. Living outside the cocoon of familiarity had been my first act of rebellion, a silent declaration of independence that had laid the groundwork for the audacious leap I was now contemplating.

Despite their objections, I stood firm in my resolve. I listened to their concerns and acknowledged them respectfully, but deep down, I knew I had to follow my own path. I had often daydreamed about what other parts of the world looked and sounded like, even the way other nationalities related to each other. Some may believe that's the purpose of television and the Internet, but I desired to experience those things firsthand. I knew there was more to life than the few states I had visited or resided.

Growing up a tad bit sheltered in the North American South, my exposure to diversity was limited. Sure, I had seen glimpses of exotic destinations on screen and heard foreign languages spoken through the speakers of my television and stages of great playwrights, but it was all a distant vision, an enticing, yet unattainable dream. So, when the opportunity rose to step outside the confines of my comfort zone and immerse myself in a world unknown, I seized it, determined to turn my daydreams into reality. I sensed the promise of growth, of discovery, of a life lived not just within the confines of expectation, but on the untamed frontier of possibility. It wasn't about rebellion or defiance; it was about honoring the voice within me that yearned for something more, something beyond the confines of tradition and expectation.

As I prepared to embark on this new chapter of my life in the United Arab Emirates (UAE), I braced myself for the repercussions of my decision. I knew there would be whispers of dissent among other family members, raised eyebrows from coworkers, and perhaps even judgmental glances from friends. But I didn't care. I was doing it anyway! This was my journey, my choice, and I was determined to see it through despite any external opinions.

Raised as a Southern girl, I was instilled with the values of helping those in need and giving back to the community. From a young age, it was ingrained in me that with fortune and blessings came responsibility. I needed to use my skillsets and education to make a positive impact. But for once in my life, I was going to prioritize my own desires and ambitions.

This decision wasn't about selfishness; it was about self-discovery and empowerment. I was finally leveraging my expensive-ass education, professional experience, and unique skillsets for myself. It was time to break free from the constraints of convention and carve out my own path, one that resonated with my innermost desires and aspirations. And, as I took that bold step forward, I embraced the uncertainty of the journey ahead, knowing it was mine, and mine alone, to navigate.

Liberating myself from the well-worn path of selfless service, I resolved to pursue my own ambitions. As I ignored the whispers of doubt and the echoing voices of tradition, I stood firm in the belief that my unique blend of education and experience could pave the way for a fulfilling and unconventional adventure.

With my two-year contract signed, documents and degrees authenticated, and visa approved, the day finally arrived. I was moving to the Middle East with four suitcases and a bookbag. In that moment, as I boarded the plane bound for a foreign land, I realized I was no longer bound by the expectations of others. I was charting my own course, guided by the inner compass of my dreams and aspirations.

Though the journey ahead would be fraught with challenges and uncertainty, I knew I was finally living life on my own terms. I was taking the road less traveled, and reminded myself to keep an open mind about the experiences to follow.

My international traveling expeditions started in the summer of 2009, the last year of the 2000s decade, which was proclaimed the International Year of Reconciliation. The motto was "Unity and Diversity". To everything there is a season and a time to every purpose. How much more serendipitous could it get than that?

The Profession

I became an educator after having served my country in the U.S. Army and returning to the Army to work as a civilian in the computer information systems field. It was by happenstance that I became an educationalist, but I haven't looked back. I was initially certified as a special education teacher, and during my third year of teaching when the district needed to meet its quota for having English Speakers of Other Languages (ESOL) certified teachers, I was asked to consider taking the exam. The district offered to reimburse me for the exam upon successfully passing. It was the best decision I made. Having obtained my ESOL certification was my access to qualifying to teach abroad and setting the stage for international travel.

I had been teaching for about six years when I received my first unsolicited invitation to interview for a teaching job in South Korea. The interview went well, and I received an offer. However, after mentioning it to a few family members and talking with friends, I declined the offer. A few days later, my decision was still heavy on my mind, so at that moment, I promised myself that if I were to receive another offer such as this, I wouldn't turn it down. Well, who knew it would be two years later when another offer would come to me? That offer was for a lead teacher position in the United Arab Emirates. I kept my promise to myself and said, "Yes."

That ESOL certification and my yes have led me to be able to continue working abroad in various positions while exploring the world. In each country where I have lived and worked, the rules of engagement and expectations are different, but I was able to have success by always walking into a new position with open-mindedness and flexibility. The most unexpected bonus and pleasure were the students. The places I worked and lived have reared their students to be respectful to their teachers. Of course, there are naughty students everywhere, but it's tremendously different from the classrooms in the United States. Not only do the students respect their teachers, but there is an ongoing open display of appreciation and gratitude that takes place throughout the school year.

As a teacher abroad, I felt a profound sense of validation and fulfillment, knowing that my role is highly esteemed and valued. It's incredibly rewarding to be part of a society where teaching is not just seen as a job, but as a noble and honorable profession. This recognition elevates the status of educators and underscores the importance of their contribution to society.

Moreover, the continuous display of appreciation and gratitude was heartwarming and reinforced my passion for teaching. Whether it was a simple thank you from a student, a gesture of kindness from a colleague, or recognition from school administrators, the ongoing acknowledgment of our work fostered a supportive and uplifting environment.

In essence, teaching abroad afforded me a sense of pride and satisfaction in my profession. The atmosphere of respect and gratitude permeated my work, making each day in the school building a meaningful and rewarding experience.

The Travel

I'm sure you're wondering what my travels and experiences were like. Well, let me tell you they were nothing short of extraordinary! Each journey, every encounter, was a tapestry woven with threads of adventure, resilience, and profound discovery. Even when faced with challenges or what some might consider negative situations, I found that every moment presented an opportunity for growth and exploration.

Navigating as a Black woman traveling alone, reactions varied greatly across different locations, shaped by the unique blend of country, culture, and preconceived stereotypes. In some places, I was met with curiosity and genuine interest, fostering understanding and unity.

People were particularly intrigued by my natural hair and the intricate coils that seemed to defy gravity. However, as most Black women can attest, personal space, particularly when it comes to our hair, is sacred. Therefore, you can imagine the humorous yet awkward encounters that ensued when strangers, without seeking permission, and even those who expressed a desire, couldn't resist the temptation to reach out and touch my kinky coils. It was as if my hair held a magnetic allure that compelled others to reach out and explore its unique texture.

Despite the awkwardness, I couldn't help but find amusement in these situations. They were scenarios that never failed to elicit a chuckle whenever I recounted the tales to friends and family. After all, there was something undeniably comical about the universal fascination with things as mundane as the color of my skin complexion and hair density. On the other hand, there were also moments – very few – when I encountered prejudice and discrimination. While it may have been slightly uncomfortable at times, I embraced those moments of cultural exchange, attempting to foster some form of understanding and an effort to bridge the gap through shared laughter and lightheartedness.

In the end, I came to appreciate the role that my presence played in expanding others' worldviews and fostering a sense of unity amidst our differences. As I continue my journey, I carry with me the knowledge that, in some small way, I have left an indelible mark on the hearts and memories of those I encountered along the way.

In the Middle East, where relationships are considered paramount, and the phrase "Insha'Allah" (God willing) permeated every aspect of life, my interactions took on a deeply personal tone. Ninety percent of conversations revolved around sharing stories and connecting on a human level, with business matters often taking a backseat. Arabians displayed a genuine curiosity about my background, upbringing, and family.

Living in the United Arab Emirates (UAE) holds a special place in my heart, particularly because of a memorable encounter with a Sudanese colleague. Each day, we exchanged greetings in the hallways of our workplace, despite the language barrier that separated us. One day, she took the initiative to stop and engage in a conversation, despite my broken Arabic and her limited English. To my surprise and delight, she extended an invitation for me to join her family for dinner at their home. Grateful for the opportunity to experience Sudanese hospitality, I accepted her kind invitation.

As I arrived at her home, I was struck by the simplicity of the living conditions. While the structure may not have been grand, it was evident that every effort was made to maintain cleanliness and provide for the family's needs. Even with their modest means, my colleague and her family welcomed me with open arms. The aroma of delicious homemade food filled the air, and I was treated to a feast of traditional Sudanese dishes prepared with love and care.

As the evening drew to a close, my colleague insisted on packing leftovers for me to take home, insisting that I, as a single person living alone, should have a hot meal to enjoy. This gesture of generosity and kindness solidified the meaning of what it means to be grateful. Here was a family with very little wealth, yet they were willing to share what they had with a relative stranger. Forever grateful for the warmth and generosity shown to me, I left their home with a heart full of gratitude and a new-found appreciation for the beauty of shared humanity with an open heart and a willingness to embrace the kindness of others.

Now, the central question many ponder is the treatment of women and the presence of oppression in the Middle East. Undoubtedly, it's a society where men hold considerable sway. While I didn't personally feel oppressed, I did encounter limitations in my movements across certain countries. Interestingly, I came to appreciate the protective role men often assume for women, acting as their guardians and ensuring their safety.

As a single woman traveling alone, I found myself under the care of other Arab women's male companions, who took on the responsibility of looking out for me too. This included moments when strangers insisted I "get in the car" because I was walking down the street alone. Now you know, as an American, I thought they had lost their mind. I'm not doing that, but against my better judgment and *stranger danger*, I did. They took me right to my destination and drove off.

In rural areas, traditional norms and customs held firm. For instance, I had to rely on my driver to make purchases at specific restaurants since women weren't permitted to enter. There were also instances where I could enter establishments as a woman, but my driver had to accompany me inside and handle the transaction on my behalf. While these situations were frustrating at times, they highlighted the cultural nuances that shape daily life in the region.

Despite the gender dynamics, I acknowledged the reality of a male-dominated society, yet instead of feeling marginalized, I embraced the opportunity to navigate these dynamics with grace and resilience, demonstrating that strength and intellect know no gender.

In essence, my journey through the Middle East has been woven with vibrant colors of culture, hospitality, and personal growth, gaining a deeper understanding of the richness and complexity of the region. This region is where I created some of my fondest memories abroad. It will always be my original home away from home.

Moving eastward to Southeast Asia, I was transported back to my experiences in the Middle East as I navigated through its bustling streets, explored vibrant markets, and immersed myself in the culture. It is a beautiful land to explore, where most of the countries' streets are very clean and the people take pride in their work and accomplishments. And while the landscapes, religion, and traditions varied, there were intriguing similarities in the demeanor and attitudes of the people that caught my attention.

I encountered a notable sense of assertiveness and in-dependence, particularly among women, which reso-nated with me. But what stood out most was the wel-coming atmosphere that allowed me to feel comfortable exploring.

I traversed through the serene greenery of Brunei's rain-forests while living and working in the country. I ex-plored the ancient temples of Cambodia, the bustling streets of Jakarta, and the tranquil charm of Laos. Then there's Malaysia, where the airport is literally its own shopping mall. Singapore has modern marvels of steel and luxuries to enjoy while breathing clean air. Thailand is full of fun mixed in with some surprises and every-one is free to be them, while Vietnam holds a history of war and untold stories of its wartime plight. It also in-cludes fantasy world parks, beaches, and a mighty fash-ion industry.

All of these traveling senses sharply contrast with my experiences in Western Asian countries, where my ar-rival seemed to trigger prejudiced assumptions and ste-reotyping. From the moment I stepped foot in Western Asia, I felt the weight of judgment and the impact of media-driven perceptions shaping how I was viewed. This manifested in uncomfortable encounters such as mocking laughter, intrusive photography, and a palpable sense of apprehension in the air. These barriers hindered genuine interaction and left me feeling isolated, unable to bridge the divide.

In Europe, I encountered the enduring challenges of racism and segregation, similar to my experiences in the United States. Although progress may seem evident on the surface, these issues linger beneath a veneer of friendliness and charm, particularly noticeable in tourist settings.

As an American tourist, I have enjoyed pleasant experiences shielded by the sometimes superficial hospitality. Conversations with Europeans often carried an undertone of condescension, seemingly deeming my perspective inferior. I occasionally felt patronized, a subtle but clear indication of the belittlement and elitism that pervaded these interactions. However, I also had great conversations while exploring tourist sites with fellow travelers.

Touring European countries was like embarking on a journey through time and culture. My explorations have shown to be a treasure trove of art, history, and natural beauty, with iconic landmarks like the Eiffel Tower and Acropolis, medieval castles, and scenic coastlines. Ultimately, I plan to explore more of this continent and look forward to my combined experiences being enriched.

And then, there is Africa, which sadly remains one of the least explored destinations in my travels, although I've had the privilege of connecting with Africans who now reside in other parts of the world. When I stepped foot on the rich soils of Ethiopia, Egypt, and Ghana, I understood that I was gaining valuable insights into the behaviors and interactions of Black individuals in America, shedding light on the cultural bonds that unite us across continents. These encounters felt like reuniting with long-lost family or cherished friends, deepening my understanding of cultural nuances and shared experiences within the African diaspora.

The cultural values and traditions that permeate African societies reverberate deeply with me, emphasizing manners, respect, and hospitality. From the simple gestures of saying "excuse me," "please," and "thank you," to the generosity extended to guests, these customs mirror the values instilled in many Black communities in America. It serves as a poignant reminder of the enduring legacy of African heritage and the diverse cultural practices that shape our collective identity.

Despite prevalent stereotypes and misconceptions, Africa's reality is nuanced and diverse, far beyond what mainstream media often portrays. The continent's terrain embodies a blend of contrasts and complexities, from bustling urban centers with modern infrastructure, to remote villages with traditional dwellings. Africa's rich history, woven with both triumphs and tragedies, serves as a reminder of the resilience and strength of its people. In essence, Africa is a mosaic of cultures, landscapes, and histories, rivaling any other region on Earth in its diversity and complexity. My travels and connections with individuals of African descent have allowed me to appreciate the multifaceted beauty of the continent and its enduring significance in shaping the global narrative of humanity.

The Nomad's Reflections

"It's about time you came home," my father said. "And don't be trying to rush back over there either!" my mother added.

Ironically, the first time I returned home after my extended stint living abroad, I was taken aback by two things. First was the reaction to my parents' comments. I had spent years abroad, living my life to the fullest, meeting people, trying new things, and seeing parts of the world that very few in my family had explored. Yet, in the end, all they cared about was the fact that I was back on American soil.

The second surprise was when I heard someone remark that I had changed. At first, I felt a twinge of offense, as if my core identity had been called into question. But upon deeper reflection, I realized that perhaps I had indeed undergone some transformation during my time away, and that was perfectly alright. In fact, I began to embrace the idea that my experiences abroad had likely shaped me into a better version of myself.

Since then, my thirst for exploration has only intensified. I've had the privilege of venturing to thirty-two countries spread across three continents, journeys that have broadened my horizons in countless ways. Moving about the globe, visiting renowned architectural marvels, groundbreaking landmarks, and ancient wonders was astounding, but what truly stuck with me was not the sights, but the interactions I had with people. Regardless of the grandeur of the locations or the significance of these monuments, it was the relationships and memories we created that have made a lasting impact.

Indeed, it's true that negative experiences can happen anywhere. However, I chose to approach my travels with an open heart and a positive outlook. This has afforded the discovery that kindness knows no borders and genuine warmth and hospitality can be found in the most unexpected places.

I look forward to the adventures that lie ahead as I set out to add more stamps to my passport and expand my network of fellow travelers. Travel, for me, goes beyond ticking off destinations on a list; it's about the discovery of new cultures, forming deep connections with people from diverse backgrounds, and constantly pushing my boundaries.

Having worked abroad as an educator, my career has not only provided me with the opportunity to make a positive impact through teaching and mentorship, but has also enabled me to fulfill my wanderlust and explore the world on my own terms. By combining my passion for education with my love of travel, I've been able to create

a lifestyle that allows me to pursue my interests and aspirations while also making a difference in the lives of
others. It's a rewarding and fulfilling way to live, and I
am grateful for those opportunities that my career has
afforded me.

In the wise words of Mae West, "You only live once, but
if you do it right, once is enough." And so, armed with a
sense of adventure and a soul longing to travel, I embark
on each new journey with gratitude and excitement, ea-
ger to make the most of this one precious life.

Acknowledgments

"United, women have the power to create a tidal wave of change, sweeping away barriers and forging new paths toward equality and empowerment."

My Sorors, Tiffanie Barner-Davis and Yvonne Mahoney, who had the courage to speak their truth and put it in writing, I think you're both amazing, brave, and courageous! This project was meant for many, but it now encompasses those it was meant to be for. Congratulations to you.

Special thanks to my friend, Soror, Sister, and editor, Rhonda Lawson, for your tireless advocacy and belief in this project from its inception. I made one phone call and shared my idea, and you said, "Oh, that's easy! I got you." Thanks for always answering the call and bringing this book to fruition.

Lastly, I want to express my appreciation to the readers who will embark on this journey with us as you turn the pages. Your support and enthusiasm mean the world to us. I appreciate each and every one of you.

From Grief to Life

By

Yvonne Mahoney

This is dedicated to the C.A.G. Divas and my God-given family. I love you with my heart. Smooches!

Grief is defined in the Oxford dictionary as "deep sorrow, especially that caused by someone's death."

My sister/friend transitioned. Was this real, or was I dreaming? How would I handle this? How would I move forward without her?

That was a pivotal moment in my life. I didn't imagine she would transition. I imagined us "mature", sitting on a porch drinking whatever and reminiscing about the past. There were three of us sister/friends celebrating a milestone that year. We planned on celebrating together by going on a trip, maybe going on a cruise or, perhaps, Paris, France. I had never been on a cruise so that would have been my choice. None of us had been to Paris so that would have been a good choice for all of us.

I was looking forward to going because we had never been on a trip together, but that plan was altered. That milestone year, my sister/friend was ill, so the plans were put on hold. I was also being ordained as an elder in The Lord's Church that year, which was an important moment in my life. I wanted her to be there, but that plan was also altered. By the time the date for my ordination came, she had transitioned. Why did this happen? Why was it her? It felt it wasn't fair. It wasn't time. But who am I to feel this way?

The friendship with my sister/friend started in the ninth

grade (will not reveal the year—LOL!) at Burke High School in Charleston, South Carolina. We found ourselves in the same homeroom and most of the same classes. For some reason we gravitated toward each other. We would have conversations and we would study together. It got to the point when you saw her, you would see me.

We lived near each other, so we walked home together. We did a lot of things together, like going to football games, dressing alike, making clothes, and visiting each other's houses. I fondly remember making matching outfits in Home Economics (remember that class?) to wear to Homecoming. We made blue and white polka dot hip hugger pants! When I tell you those pants turned out awesome! We were some bad mamma jammas at that Homecoming game!

We also attended the same church, so we participated in Junior Church, where the young people of the church would get together on a Thursday evening and do basically Bible study and other activities. Church was an interesting dynamic. Once we got to high school, the young people would sit upstairs. To this day I do not know why, but we were happy that we were able to sit up there and talk (which we should not have been doing). I guess that was also teenage church! The funniest thing was we always knew when the pastor was wrapping up the sermon because he would do the same move every time. We thought that was entertaining!

When we started hanging out outside of school, this friendship was born. We would meet and go to the battery, a Sunday hang out spot, and meet up with other classmates and just talk and people watch. We also double-dated a few times. Some of those times, she provided the date! LOL! I'm not saying all those dates she provided were successful, but most of the time they were fun.

She was in my life longer than any romantic relationship. My sister/friend was always there to let me know if I was making the right decision, but even if I went against her advice, she supported me anyway. Now, that's how you know you have a real sister/friend. We got into quite a few situations back in the day. If I tell all the shenanigans we got into, I will have to—well, you know the saying. LOL!

My sister/friend also came to visit me the first time I attempted to attend college. I know she enjoyed herself because it was Homecoming, and that was always a good time. It was always a good time when we got together.

At one point, we did lose contact with each other, but after that separation, we were back together like no time passed.

Fast forward to 2016. We hadn't talked in a while (we would try to talk at least once a month). I was scrolling Facebook as I usually do and saw a picture of my sister/friend in a hospital bed. I was shocked, to say the least. I reached out to her, and she knew exactly why I was calling.

Side note: I really dislike finding out news about my friends on social media. Okay, on with the story.

I found out my sister/friend's brother-in-law posted that picture without her permission. She didn't know about it being on Facebook until someone told her. Once she found out, she knew she had to tell me what was going on. As you can imagine, she was upset because she wasn't a person to share her business on Facebook. Her brother-in-law eventually took it down, but not before some people had seen it.

My sister/friend explained what was going on and said it was nothing to worry about. When she received her test results, she called and let me know she had been diagnosed with seizures and was given a prescription to control them. Other than that, she was okay, and everything was normal. If she was not that concerned, then I wouldn't stress about it.

As time went on, we talked occasionally and all was well, or so I thought. One day, I received a call from her phone. When I answered, it was her son, who informed me that my sister/friend was in the hospital. I was shocked.

Sometimes when you're ill, the quality of care you receive depends on the hospital you go to, who you are, and if you have insurance. Again, my sister/friend was diagnosed with and treated for seizures, but the seizures progressively got worse. The treatment wasn't working, and she wasn't getting any relief. Her sons and sister decided my sister/friend wasn't getting the proper care and decided to have her moved to another hospital.

When she arrived at the second hospital, the seizures still got progressively worse, so the doctors kept her sedated. After a series of tests, it was determined she had a rare condition called SPS, or Stiff Person Syndrome (only my sister/friend would have a rare condition). According to the Johns Hopkins Medicine website, SPS is a rare autoimmune neurological disorder that most commonly causes muscle stiffness and painful spasms that come and go and can worsen over time. So, she wasn't having seizures; they were muscle spasms and rigidity related to SPS.

I decided to start visiting her so I could see her and get information firsthand. I visited her for the first time in November 2016. That first visit was exceedingly difficult. You see, my sister/friend was full of life and always the life of the party. She was a giant social butterfly, always joking and wanting to see the best in people. But don't get it twisted. She had that other side you didn't want to mess with. She was a true Gemini!

Seeing my sister/friend just lying there hooked up to all those tubes and wires with a machine helping her breathe was unsettling, to say the least. I did all I could not to break down in tears right there. That visual stays with me to this day. The only thing I could do was sit there and be present. At that time, the visitors were limited, so waiting until someone left the room was also challenging. I was ready to see her, but I had to wait. It was taxing on my emotions, and it took me a while to work through that. The next time I went to see her, she would wake up and go back to sleep. That was slightly encouraging and made me feel hopeful. There was less she was hooked to, but she was still sedated, which was still not a good sight. I don't know if she was aware I was there; I would hope she did. For most of the visit, I conversed with the friend who came with me, or with other visitors who dropped in while I was there. It seemed as though she was progressing every time I visited, like she was moving forward with her healing.

The third time I visited, my sister/friend was breathing on her own and recognizing people! Man, I was a happy person! It was very uplifting to see her with this progress! She couldn't speak, but she would use her facial expressions and mouth what she wanted. I stayed for a while watching TV with her, and a few times she laughed. That visit really encouraged me. It made me feel like things were going to be okay. When I left, I told her I would be back soon, and expected to see her sitting up and talking. Then something happened that made my soul leap. My sister/friend moved her lips and asked me to pray for her. Let me tell you how that affected me! My spirit ran into the hallway and did a holy dance! Have you ever had that experience? Whew! But physically, I grabbed her hand and prayed a prayer like never before. She was shocked because she probably meant she wanted me to remember her in prayer, but the Spirit said pray right then! She thanked me, and I told her I loved her. When I left that hospital, I just knew she would eventually be going home. It may have been a long recovery, but at least she would be on the way to healing. Little did I know she was going home, but not her home on Rutledge Avenue.

It was Sunday, and my brother and I were on our way home from church. We stopped to take home some food to eat so we could wind down from church. Usually, I drive, but this Sunday, he drove us home. My phone rang. When I saw my sister/friend's number, I just knew the news would be that she was being released from the hospital, but when I answered and heard her son's voice, my heart knew what he would say. My sister/friend transitioned April 2, 2017, at 3 p.m. If I had been driving the car, that news may have caused an accident. I was just there a little over a week before, and now she was with the ancestors looking out for us. I was utterly shocked and devastated.

I tell you my faith was so strong that I believed with everything in me that my sister/friend would leave that hospital. I was truly walking by faith, as the scripture says in II Corinthians 5:7 NKJV: "For we walk by faith, and not by sight." I wasn't going by how my sister/friend looked lying in that bed because if I did, I would have had no faith whatsoever. My faith was so strong that I believed we would celebrate our milestone birthdays together. Although we may not have been able to take that trip we were planning at that time, we would have been able to celebrate. My faith was so strong that I believed she would make a full recovery and be able to live a full life. But that turned out not to be the plan. Even though that was not the result, my faith was not shaken. She did recover, but not in the way we thought.

Grief is a tricky thing. There are so many things that go with grief. You know the five stages of grief—denial, anger, bargaining, depression, and acceptance. I would add my own stage –devastation. Let us look at these stages of grief: Denial: "failure to acknowledge an unacceptable truth or emotion, or to admit it into consciousness, used as a defense mechanism". Transition of a loved one would be an unacceptable truth. It's like you believe a truth is a lie, but it's really the truth. It's confusing and can take you into a tailspin. It's like being in shock, but not realizing you are. You walk around shaking your head in disbelief. It hasn't sunk in yet.

Anger: "is a human emotion that involves intense displeasure"

Anger is an emotion that can take you to head spaces that can be detrimental to your health. Anger will make you take things out on people who didn't do anything but try to help you. And unbelievably, it will make you be angry with God. You blame God for what happened to your loved one. You don't want to hear about God, you don't want to pray, or have anyone pray for you. You could even turn your back on God (or however you refer to your higher power). Anger can be dangerous if you don't know how to handle it or get help with it. It can consume you and turn you into someone you aren't. If anger takes over, that is a sign the professional help is needed.

Bargaining: "to arrive at (an agreement or settlement)"

When you hear the word bargaining, you wouldn't think it would be an emotion related to grief, but it is. Most of the time, you would think the bargaining would take place before your loved one transitions, but it also happens during the grief process. It comes with wondering what would have happened if there had been a different plan. You go back into your thoughts and wonder if you should have done something differently. You wonder if you prayed enough or visited enough. Sometimes this stage can also overtake your thoughts. Always remember, there is help to work through grief.

Depression: "a state of feeling sad-low spirits"
Depression can creep up at any time. At first, it may seem as though you're not depressed because you feel sad. Of course, sadness is normal because you are missing someone who has been part of your life. You always hear it gets better with time and you wonder how much time. Depression is like the waves of the ocean, with ebbs and tides, calm and waves. You could be calm for days or months, and then overwhelming sadness comes out of the blue. You would think that would be a normal process until one or two days turn into a week, and then weeks. The next thing you know, a couple of months have gone by and you haven't shaken that feeling of

overwhelming sadness. You wonder how you got this far, and how you can get out. There are several ways to come out of depression. Some people use church as a way out of depression. Some people go to therapy to work through their depression. Some people use meditation or Reiki. Any or all of these can be used to help get you out of the pit of depression.

Acceptance: "the act of assenting or believing" Finally, there is acceptance. Out of all the stages of grief, this may be the most difficult. At this point, some time probably has gone by. You are at the point where you have come to the realization that your loved one is with the ancestors. You really don't want to accept it, but it's time for you to try. It's painful at first, but as you ease yourself into acceptance, the pain subsides slowly. It doesn't fully go away, but it doesn't hurt as much as it did in the beginning. You are beginning to accept the change of life while missing your loved one.

Devastation: "to overwhelm, as with grief or dismay"

I added devastation because that is how I felt. I'm sure others have felt that way and didn't really know how to describe the feeling. It sort of puts all the emotions together. We have no energy, and are sleeping or eating more than usual, or not at all. Some turn to drinking excessively to numb the pain or abusing prescription or non-prescription drugs.

Devastation can cause all of those symptoms, and, if not controlled, it also can cause your life to spiral out of control. You would hope it doesn't lead to anything detrimental, but it can. Hopefully, family and friends will care enough to reach out to make sure you are healing. As for me, I didn't go through denial, bargaining, or acceptance. However, that anger and depression were the ones, along with my added stage of devastation. I can attest I was angry at the situation—not my sister/ friend or God. I was angry because I wasn't there to say goodbye. I was angry because I felt she didn't get the proper initial care or diagnosis. I was angry because my heart was hurt.

I was depressed for a long time. It wasn't a deep depression, but I recognized it was depression. The reason I feel I didn't go through acceptance is because I'm not sure I have accepted it. For me to accept the situation means I have to let go, and I'm not quite sure I'm ready to let go. When I got that call, I was immediately devastated. I hadn't felt that type of devastation and pain since my mother transitioned. I could hardly pull myself together. I had to sit in the car because I couldn't move. I cried while my brother attempted to console me. He even started praying for me and being patient. I had to find the positive in that moment. I visited her in the hospital, I kept updated through her sons, and I continuously prayed for her. Thinking about those things helped me get out of the car. Thinking about those things helped me call our other two sister/friends to give them the news. Thinking about those things helped me eat the meal I had just purchased. I was devastated, but I still had to go to work the next day. I had to tell my supervisor I would need to be off due to her transition and I would be attending the homegoing service. Repeating my sister/friend had transitioned was challenging to say out loud. It was like if I didn't say it out loud it wasn't true.

The time between my sister/friend's transition and the day of her wake and homegoing celebration was nerve wrecking. It again took me back to the time my mother transitioned. The anticipation of seeing her for the final time wasn't something I wanted to experience. However, it was something I needed to do for myself and to honor her life. It would lead to starting to be able to accept the fact she wasn't physically present.

I didn't know what to expect or how I would react. I appreciated the fact that I wasn't going to be alone. I went with my other sister/friend who was having the milestone birthday.

The wake was beautiful, and the homegoing was lively and represented her well. It was sad, but it wasn't heavy. People said beautiful things about her, and she looked beautiful. More people had stories and memories that attested that she lived life fully.

The repast after the service was like a family reunion. I saw classmates and friends I hadn't seen in years. As she often did in life, my sister/friend had gathered us together. It was another testament to her personality and love for people.

After traveling to Charleston, South Carolina to celebrate the life of my sister/friend, it was time to come to the reality that I wouldn't be able to have a long conversation with my sister/friend. We talked about some things of importance, and we talked about silly things. We talked about politics, family, and God. We even had Bible study together. We laughed, we cried and made our opinion known, but never once disrespected each other. I could no longer visit her and go have a meal, an adult beverage, laugh and act silly.

The reality was we wouldn't celebrate our milestone birthdays together. The reality was we wouldn't be able to take that international trip we always talked about. The reality was I couldn't call and ask her about someone in our class. She knew most things happening in our hometown of Charleston. The reality was my sister/friend was no longer physically present. That was a hard pill to swallow.

I struggled for a long time to adjust to the fact that I couldn't make that phone call. There were several times I pulled up her name in my phone to call and had to remind myself I couldn't talk to her. I would listen to her voicemail just to hear her voice. She was so much a part of my life, and still is to this day. I still miss her immensely. I have adjusted, but birthdays, holidays, and the transition anniversaries have been difficult.

At one point in my journey, I saw a therapist for other situations I was going through. In one session, I expressed how I felt about my sister/friend's and mother's transitions. They were both significant moments in my life. My therapist gave me suggestions on how to deal with the emotions. For instance, she suggested I celebrate those occasions by releasing balloons in their honor. I didn't do that because where I reside, it could cause issues with aviation. Instead, I post pictures and a heart-felt message on Facebook on my sister/friend's birthday and transition anniversary.

Most of the time, this helps. But then there are those times that it doesn't really help. In those cases, I just work through the emotions with whatever it takes, even if it's crying or just not doing anything. I have learned that this is okay. As the saying goes, it is okay not to be okay. Just don't stay there. Move forward and keep healing.

Through all of this, I have learned some things. The saying life is short is a true statement. I have learned to live life and enjoy every moment. By no means am I saying it has been an easy process. However, I have learned to enjoy life more. For instance, I decided to take that birthday trip I had already planned. I started not to take the trip, but it didn't make sense to cancel. My sister/friend would not have wanted me to do that. So, I went on my birthday trip to New Orleans and genuinely enjoyed myself, and even lit a candle at a local church in my sister/friend's memory.

Since my sister/friend's transition, I have also become more spontaneous. I used to be a stickler for planning, but I opened myself up for spontaneity. I have had some great moments doing things on the spot. For instance, my brother is a flight attendant. One day, we talked about just getting on a flight and having a meal in a different city for the day. I said I would be open to that. Normally I wouldn't even think of doing something like that, but my new outlook on life made me look through different lenses. So, the next thing I knew, my brother invited me to Detroit to have lunch. So, we got on a flight and spent the day in Detroit. I would have never done that before my new outlook on life.

I also learned to take advantage of opportunities. The same year my sister/friend transitioned, my job at the time offered an opportunity to finish my bachelor's degree. I'd always wanted to finish but didn't have the finances to complete it. So, when Ashford University formed a partnership with my job to offer degree programs, it piqued my interest. I spoke with a counselor and got the specifics.

It was feasible, but I almost talked myself out of it. I thought I was too mature to study from home. I didn't think I had the discipline to complete it. However, I thought about it and concluded I would be the same age at the end whether I pursued it or not, so I went for it. It was a struggle because working and going to school is no joke. And the funny thing is, I'm not a fan of reading uninteresting books! But, I could hear my sister/friend saying, "Girl, you better go ahead. You can do it!"

So, in 2017, I started the journey of obtaining my bachelor's degree. In 2020, I received my bachelor's degree in accounting from Ashford University. I don't know if I would have achieved that if my sister/friend hadn't transitioned. Thank you, sis, even though you weren't physically present.

I had also always wanted to be part of a sorority. Now that I had my degree, I was qualified to join, but certainly I was too mature at that point to achieve that. I decided anyway to do my research and found that I wanted to be part of Zeta Phi Beta Sorority, Incorporated. I asked a friend who was a Zeta how to become a member. I attended an interest meeting and immediately became interested. I went through the process, and later became a member of Zeta Phi Beta Sorority, Incorporated. I don't know if that would have happened if my sister/friend hadn't transitioned. So, thank you, sis, even though you were not physically present.

The road from grief to life has not been a straight path. There have been twists, turns, peaks, and valleys, but there is life after grief. You just have to be willing to put in the work and keep the faith. Don't wait until things are in order to live life.

As long as you have breath and health, there is an opportunity to bring your dreams to life. In no way am I saying it's easy. On the other hand, it may be easy. Either way, don't let it stop your dream. You were given the dream because you can handle it. Nothing is impossible if you have faith.

"Faith is taking the first step even when you don't see the whole staircase."

Rev. Dr. Martin L. King, Jr.

Acknowledgments

This project started as a paragraph and turned into a love story about a beautiful friend. I wanted to do this to honor her and our sister/friendship. I have been a member of Zeta Phi Beta Sorority Incorporated, Alpha Alpha Kappa Zeta chapter in Newnan, Ga for three years. I would like to acknowledge and thank Dr.

Lynèa Laws, who challenged me to complete this project. I would also like to thank La Shonda Latham and Tiffanie Barner-Davis for their encouragement.

About the Authors

Tiffanie Davis

Tiffanie Barner-Davis, a seasoned educator with over two decades of experience, is fueled by a relentless commitment to lifelong learning. Presently, she holds the position of Academic Content Lead for Elementary English Language Arts in Clayton County Public Schools. In addition to her role in the educational system, she has embarked on her own venture, founding G.I.F.T. Educational Consulting, aimed at enhancing the instructional methods of fellow educators.

Recognized twice as Teacher of the Year, Tiffanie boasts a spectrum of certifications in her field, including reading specialist, gifted education, ESOL, leadership, and teacher support and coaching. Her mission is to foster environments where individuals are encouraged to think critically and engage in collaborative discourse as they delve into new realms of knowledge.

In her capacity as a facilitator, Tiffanie orchestrates professional learning opportunities, where her fervor for enriching the lives of others shines through. She is driven by a personal commitment to empower individuals with transformative knowledge, both in their personal and professional spheres. This dedication propels her to mentor, consult, and collaborate with educators on their growth journeys, while also nurturing a supportive community for open communication, growth, and flourishing.

Creativity runs deep in Tiffanie's veins. Her passion for music has seen her lend her voice to various choirs and contribute background vocals to diverse projects. Writing, too, holds a special place in her heart, and she seamlessly integrates it into the educational experiences she crafts for diverse audiences.

At the core of her philosophy is a belief in leading with love. Tiffanie's approach is rooted in a genuine desire to understand others first, allowing her to positively influence the growth of both herself and those around her.

Dr. Lynéa Laws

Lynéa N. Laws is an international educator, leader, author, and entrepreneur. She firmly believes that every individual should live their life's purpose, and, in doing so, it takes surrounding yourself with like-minded individuals, failures, tenacity, and a plan.

Her academic journey includes a bachelor's degree in computer information systems from the University of Mary Hardin-Baylor, a master's in education from Tarleton State University, and a Ph.D. in leadership from Capella University. Dr. Laws' commitment to education led her to pursue a teaching certificate in special education, furthering her impact both in and out of the classroom. Since receiving her certification, she has served the education community both inside and outside the classroom by teaching and conducting professional development training throughout several school systems and internationally.

Outside of her educational pursuits, Lynéa is highly

engaged in community service, actively volunteering for numerous non-profit organizations, and serving on their boards in various capacities. Her commitment to giving back extends to her involvement as a member of Zeta Phi Beta Sorority, Incorporated, where she contributes her time and expertise to support its mission and initiatives. Through her dedication to philanthropy and service, Lynéa demonstrates her unwavering commitment to making a positive impact in our world.

Yvonne Mahoney

Yvonne Mahoney was born and raised in Charleston, South Carolina. She was educated in the schools of Charleston and graduated from the High School of Charleston.

Yvonne lived in Charlotte, North Carolina for several years, but after visiting home one year, she decided to move back home to be near her parents. While living in Charleston, she decided to go to school to get her degree, and attended Trident Technical College, where she received her associate degree in accounting.

Later in life, she moved to Atlanta, Georgia and is currently living there. After some time, an opportunity was afforded to complete her degree and she took advantage of it. She started attending Ashford University (which is now known as UAGC), and received her bachelor's degree in accounting.

She is also a member of the beloved Zeta Phi Beta

Sorority Incorporated, Alpha Alpha Kappa Zeta chapter in Newnan, Georgia.

Yvonne loves sports, especially the Carolina Panthers, Charlotte Hornets, and Atlanta Braves. She loves traveling, movies, and games to keep the mind sharp.

"And we know that all things work together for good to those who love God, to those who are called according to His purpose."

- Romans 8:28